The Baseball Haggadah

A Festival of Freedom and Springtime in 15 Innings

Then the Eternal took us out of Mitzrayim with a mighty hand
and an outstretched arm, with awesome power,
and with signs and wonders.
—Deuteronomy 26:8

By Rabbi Sharon G. Forman
Illustrated by Lisa J. Teitelbaum

Scarsdale, New York

TABLE OF CONTENTS

Foreword

Game 5 of the 1999 National League Championship Series was played between the New York Mets and rival club, Atlanta Braves. We stood together that night at Shea Stadium, along with the 55,723 fans in attendance, witness to Mets' third baseman, Robin Ventura's, bases-loaded walk-off grand slam single in the bottom of the 15th inning. The already excited crowd roared as soon as Ventura's bat made contact with the ball, sending it over the right field wall. Knowing that we had witnessed a significant moment in baseball history, we joined in as the fans cheered loudly, and Ventura's teammates celebrated with him around second base, not allowing him to advance to home plate, and thus forcing his "grand slam single."

That historic night was also significant in the development of our relationship as brothers. Born ten years apart, it took some time for us to come together as friends, and baseball became a common interest for us to share. The crowd at a baseball game represents a unique cross section of our community. You see young and old, friends and family, co-workers and strangers—all united by a shared energy. It is a snapshot of the larger American society, and a symbol our our country's identity. Baseball has the gift of uniting us, across culture, ethnicity, religion and age.

We are both delighted to come together on this project, one that marries baseball and Judaism. This Haggadah allows us to experience the story of Israel's Exodus from Egypt through the lens of the modern baseball fan. The Passover *seder* is the ultimate post-game wrap, transporting attendees back in time to witness Moses' transition from Prince of Egypt to messenger of God and deliverer of the People of Israel. As we read each year on Passover, *B'chol dor vador chayav adam lirot et atzmo k'ilu hu yatza mi-Mitzrayim*, "In every generation a person is obligated to look at himself as if he personally had gone out of Egypt" *(Pesachim 116b)*. We do not just tell the story of our Exodus from Egypt, but rather re-experience the saga and identify with the poor and downtrodden slaves in Egypt. This Haggadah packages the experience in a way that is accessible and fun for baseball lovers like us!

Chag Sameach!

Jon "JD" Daniels
President of Baseball Operations
& General Manager, Texas Rangers

Ryan E. Daniels
Rabbinical Student, Hebrew Union College - Jewish Institute of Religion, New York

January 2015 / *Tevet 5775*

Acknowledgements

Gratitude is a major theme of the Festival of Passover. We are grateful for our freedom, for the rebirth of springtime, and for the opportunity to reach this season once again. I am deeply grateful to my friend and the illustrator of this project, Lisa Teitelbaum, who has breathed life into this Haggadah with color, wit, and beauty. Her encouragement and intelligence have elevated this project on every level. Vivian Singer has lent her expertise in computers, publishing, and liturgy to serve as a compassionate and wise midwife to this project.

Thanks are also due to my informal editorial committee comprised of Jewish educators and clergy, baseball professionals, and seder veterans who appreciate the twisted beauty of a tortured pun and an unexpected double play. You have given me the gift of your time, knowledge, and enthusiasm. Many thanks to my siblings, Dr. Julie Forman-Kay, Rabbi Joseph Forman, and Cantor Alisa Forman; and my friends and colleagues, soon-to-be-Rabbi Ryan Daniels, Jon Daniels, Reyna Marder Gentin, Randi Karmen Guttenberg, Kim Hoelting, Rabbi Valerie Lieber, Steve Pinto, Jeffrey Rothschild, and Rich Wurtzburger.

This project would not have been conceived without the insight of my son, Josh Marx. Abigail, Joshua, and Benjamin are my inspiration for testing new ideas and sharing my love of Judaism. And of course, thanks to my husband, Steven Marx, for being my ultimate catch and for encouraging me to let this unconventional project take flight. I am fortunate to be on the same team as all of you.

I must mention my grandfather of blessed memory, Joseph Meyer Fish, whom I never had the opportunity to meet, but whose enduring love of baseball and even greater devotion to Jewish learning have been passed down through the generations and have found some expression in the pages of this Haggadah and in the hearts of his great-grandchildren. How I wish that together we could have watched your beloved Dodgers play a baseball game or shared even one seder. Although not a field of dreams in Iowa, perhaps this Haggadah allows us to do a bit of both.

Rabbi Sharon G. Forman

Introduction for Adults and Seder Coaches

Why is this night different from all other nights of the year? And what does the game of baseball have to do with the Festival of Passover and the seder, the celebratory Passover meal and retelling of the story of the Jewish people's liberation from slavery? For years we have been singing questions and answers about matzah, bitter herbs, dipping foods, and the rationale for reclining at our seders. How many of us have considered that both baseball and Passover involve stories of wandering, of confronting challenges as we venture out from safety, and of finally coming home? Returning home is a group effort, but ultimately, each batter must stand alone at the plate, judging the pitches, and making his or her own choices regarding when to hit and what kind of risks to take.

On Passover, we celebrate God's "mighty hand and outstretched arm" *(Deuteronomy 26:8)*. Baseball also celebrates the ability of a good arm to take a team home. One of the purposes of the Passover seder is to capture the imagination of the participants so that they may reflect on the meaning of freedom. More than an account of the Israelites' time in Egypt and their subsequent trials and return to their land, the seder is a feast in which the participants retell an ancient story, dramatically explain the meaning of specific and sometimes ingestible symbols, and ponder the various attributes of God that are extolled in the Haggadah.

Over the centuries, rabbis designed the seder to remind us that it was not only sunburned, old Israelite relatives down in Egypt who witnessed God's redemption. The Exodus is an ongoing experience that continues today: "You have seen all that the Eternal did before your own eyes in the land of Egypt to Pharaoh and to all his servants and to all his land, the great trials that your own eyes have seen, those great signs and portents" *(Deuteronomy 29:1-2)*. We may find the seder a compelling experience, as it celebrates freedom, overcoming personal and communal difficulties, and looking toward a future filled with promise and peace. The historically hazy tale of 600,000 newly freed Israelites wandering through the desert thousands of years ago prompts us to reflect on our ideas about ethical labor markets, diplomacy, politics, and the role of a deity who may or may not intervene in the course of history. Our seders crackle with excitement when we infuse an old ritual with thought provoking readings and bring new insights and interpretations to our table. Especially when children are present, we have opportunities to shake out old matzah crumbs from our Haggadah and approach our seder routine with a fresh perspective.

This sports oriented Haggadah is designed for lovers of another springtime ritual (at least in North America) — the game of baseball. Athletes and philosophers alike have written and spoken poetically about baseball's ability to tap into our connection with nature, celebrate teamwork, and invite spectators into a spirited dance of timelessness and circularity. Although the sport of baseball might have its origins in Europe, baseball is arguably the most American of sports. The innocence of teammates throwing a ball and playing tag on a green field in the summer sun is a celebration of freedom. Participants play both offense and defense; many body types can find success; and an ever-present sense of optimism permeates even the final at-bat in the last inning. A weaker team may prevail over one with stronger individual players. And there is always the joy of coming home. As baseball's seventh commissioner, A. Bartlett Giamatti, wrote, "Baseball is about going home and how hard it is to get there and how driven is our need." These themes coincide with the values celebrated at Passover.

At our family's seder, we have a custom of providing every participant with a common Haggadah and an additional alternative Haggadah to supplement his or her seder experience and that of the entire group's. From the popular varieties of chocolate Haggadah pamphlets to texts confronting serious social issues of our day, many inventive versions of this text have been crafted with the goal of motivating the participants to feel as if they had been liberated from slavery. Last Passover, at the urging of my then ten year-old son, Josh, we created our own rudimentary baseball themed Haggadah so that he and his eight year-old brother, Ben, could experience the seder with images they loved and were preoccupied with in early spring. The goal of creating this Haggadah was to infuse creativity and liveliness into a ritual that may be so habitual to an adult or so foreign to a child that it can lose its potency in touching the participants' emotions and intellect. By holding up the story of the Exodus next to the concept of a beloved national pastime, connections are made that cast light on the Passover story in new and unexpected patterns.

With a bit of imagination, home plate transforms into a seder plate, and the baseball diamond morphs into a square of matzah turned on its side. With Moses as the team captain for the Israelites and Pharaoh heading up the Taskmasters, the lineups struggle for dominance. God throws the ultimate "splitter," making way for the Israelites to cross the Sea of Reeds. Each participant takes a turn up at bat as a reader. There is a delayed 7th Inning Stretch, during which the children can go to the door to search for and welcome the presence of Elijah and Miriam. Ultimately, there is praise and joy and celebration. Freedom has been won. We, the Israelites, have made it safely home, and springtime is renewed on a field of green *karpas*. Instead of straining our eyes and scanning the stadium for Mr. Met or a favorite mascot, we will peek out of our front doors for a glimpse of Elijah the Prophet. As he turns the hearts of parents and children toward one another, we will pray for freedom for every player. It would have been enough to make it home safely, but we have been blessed to be a part of a rich tradition of beauty and justice. May this Hagaddah enchant everyone at your joyous feast, and may it enhance your seder experience. Play ball!

Coaching Tips for a Successful Seder with Young Participants: Pre-Game Warm Ups

1. Never come to a game on an empty stomach.

No matter how much fun we have spending time with family and friends around a seder table and how delicious the meal promises to be, it's always a good idea to have children come to the seder ready to pay attention, participate, and not be distracted by hunger. The seder lends itself to having plenty of hors d'oeuvres served during the KARPAS (dipping vegetables) time frame. Feel free to have a wide choice of vegetables, dips, and hardboiled eggs to stave off hunger. A little nibbling in the beginning of the seder prevents what may feel like forty years of whining in a long desert before dinner is served. Rabbinic luminaries as revered as Rabbi Akiba are cited in the Talmud suggesting that popcorn and peanuts would make an excellent snack at a seder, baseball or otherwise. In *Pesachim 108b*, our rabbis taught "we distribute to them [children] parched ears of corn and peanuts on the eve of Passover so that they should not fall asleep, and ask [the questions]."

2. It is more fun when everyone on the team has a chance to participate.

Yes, one person may be a star pitcher with her or his knowledge of Hebrew language and songs. But the seder is a team sport, and everyone present should have the chance to take a turn up at bat and participate. Children can share illustrations from their own Haggadah, sing the four questions, help hide or find the Afikoman (hidden matzah), prepare a special dish, sing a song, or even act out the plagues with puppets. Readings are divided up into small sentences and paragraphs with children's participation in mind. Older children or adults may be assigned to read the "announcers" readings, while the "batters" readings are written especially for children.

3. Teammates should know each other's names, not just jersey numbers.

Before the seder, encourage your children to create place cards for the guests. Guide your home team in folding index cards in half and writing the teammates' names. Encourage your artist helpers to create "baseball cards" for each guest. The children may also create a lineup consisting of their own dream team of players.

4. Victory requires teamwork. One team member cannot field every ball.

One of the most anticipated moments of the Passover seder occurs when the children are sent to search for the Afikoman. Unfortunately, this frenzied hunt may lead to animosity among the seekers. Instead of presenting this hunt for the Afikoman as a zero-sum-game in which only one person can emerge victorious, why not emphasize teamwork? Seder organizers may give each child an envelope labeled with the children/players' names. When the Afikoman is hidden, a piece of the dessert matzah is broken and placed into the envelopes. Just as the Afikoman represents redemption yet to come, each person must pledge to search and find her or his own piece of salvation. The seder cannot be completed until every child's piece of matzah is discovered. It's time for the meeting at the pitcher's mound, when teammates help one another settle down and get their strategy organized for a successful outing.

5. Make sure the equipment is organized and present at the game.

Just as coaches need to ensure that the field is ready for play with bases set out, the helmets placed on hooks, and extra balls available, the seder organizer needs to have all of the "equipment" prepared before the seder begins. Children can be important helpers in this task of checking off the necessary supplies and can feel more invested in the seder when they helped make it happen.

6. Make a short, but inspirational speech prior to the game.

Everyone wants to be on a winning team and to feel valued for his or her contributions. Before the seder starts, you may want to tell your participants why the seder ritual is important to you and your family and what you want to achieve. Does it remind you of time spent with a beloved relative? Do you find the themes of freedom or immigration particularly important as a Jewish person or as an American citizen? What enduring lessons do you hope to impart to your "team" by participating in this ritual?

7. Practices should be kept under two hours. Reserve the last few minutes of practices for fun games that the children enjoy.

When a seder runs much longer than your guests' attention spans, you may end up with an unscheduled game of baseball being conducted under the table. Keep your participants involved and active above the table.

8. Uniforms can add to the teams' sense of camaraderie and safety.

At your religious school model seder or Temple's "Baseball Seder," encourage attendees to wear little league jerseys or caps or *kippot* from their favorite baseball teams. With participants decked out in their baseball gear, they are psychologically primed to partake enthusiastically.

Preparing Essential Equipment for the Seder Plate and the Seder

מָרוֹר *Maror* (**Bitter Herbs**) — horseradish root, representing the bitterness of slavery

זְרוֹעַ *Z'roa* (**Roasted Shank Bone of a Lamb**) — stands for the Passover offering made at the Temple in Jerusalem or God's outstretched arm (looks a little like a baseball bat)

חֲרוֹסֶת *Charoset* — a sweet mixture of apples, nuts, wine or grape juice, and cinnamon, reminding us of the mortar of the bricks that the slaves used in Egypt (looks a little like a favorite baseball park treat of Cracker Jacks)

חֲזֶרֶת *Chazeret* — another symbol of the bitterness of slavery, usually represented by romaine lettuce or another leafy bitter vegetable and not always found on every seder plate (it's the designated hitter assisting the maror)

כַּרְפַּס *Karpas* — spring time greenery, often represented by parsley, but potatoes were used in some regions where it was difficult to find greenery in early spring (looks like a baseball field)

בֵּיצָה *Beitzah* (**Roasted Egg**) — symbol of the festival offering in the Temple and new life of spring (looks like a ball)

Salt Water — stands for the tears of the Israelites when they were slaves in Egypt. We dip the parsley into the salt water. At our Baseball Seder, it may remind us of the sweat of the baseball players in the hot sun.

מַצּוֹת ***Matzot*** — 3 matzahs, slices of unleavened bread reminding us that the Israelites left Egypt in such a hurry that their bread had no time to rise (a piece of matzah looks like a baseball diamond)

Additional Equipment for the Dugout:

Wine or Grape Juice (Kosher for Passover sports drinks): During the seder, we drink 4 cups representing joy and holiness. At the Baseball Seder, we may use a kosher for Passover sports drink.

Elijah's Cup: Everyone can fill this goblet with some grape juice or wine from his or her own cup, or the leader can put wine or grape juice in this at the start of the seder. Elijah was a prophet, or a wise person who taught people about doing the right thing. Legend teaches that on Passover, he visits everyone's seder and sips from his special cup. He is famous for watching over children and making sure everyone is getting along with each other. He is like the Commissioner of Baseball or the brave veteran honored during the game.

Cup for Miriam: This goblet is filled with water to help us remember how important Moses' sister, Miriam, was to the story of the Exodus from Egypt. She helped save Moses' life by making sure Pharaoh's daughter brought him to safety. A legend relates that wherever Miriam traveled in the desert, a well of water would appear to help refresh the Israelites. Miriam led dancing and singing at the Sea of Reeds. This is a late twentieth century addition on our seder tables and a new tradition for many families. Judaism is not only a story about boys and men. From the bravery of the midwives who rescued Jewish babies, to the bold actions of Miriam and Pharaoh's daughter, women played a crucial role in the liberation from Egypt. Girls and boys can be heroic.

Pillows: We are supposed to recline like people of leisure during the seder. Pillows even remind us of the bases on the baseball diamond. Bring your favorite baseball seat cushion to this seder.

Envelopes: Labeled with children's names for placing pieces of Afikoman (dessert matzah symbolizing hope for the future), these envelopes will keep your home free of matzah crumbs and will identify whose individual pieces of redemption belong to whom to prevent conflicts among emotional players.

Candles and Candlesticks: Not the former home of the San Francisco Giants Baseball Team, these are used to welcome the festival of Passover at the beginning of the seder.

The Innings

1. **KADESH (קַדֵּשׁ)**– Blessings Over Wine and Grape Juice
2. **URCHATZ (וּרְחַץ)**– Washing the Hands
3. **KARPAS (כַּרְפַּס)**– Vegetables
4. **YACHATZ (יַחַץ)** – Breaking the Middle Matzah
5. **MAGID (מַגִּיד)** – Retelling the Story of the Exodus
6. **RACHTZAH (רָחְצָה)**– Washing the Hands Again
7. **MOTZI (מוֹצִיא)** – First Blessings for Matzah
8. **MATZAH (מַצָּה)**– Blessing on the Matzah
9. **MAROR (מָרוֹר)**– Bitter Herb
10. **KORECH (כּוֹרֵךְ)**– Hillel Sandwich
11. **SHULCHAN ORECH (שֻׁלְחָן עוֹרֵךְ)**– Festive Meal
12. **TZAFUN** (**צָפוּן)**– The Hidden Matzah, Afikoman
13. **BARECH (בָּרֵךְ)**– Grace After Meals
14. **HALLEL (הַלֵּל)**– Hymns of Praise
15. **NIRTZAH (נִרְצָה)**– Concluding Songs

The Teams

The Israelites:

Captain: Moses

Suggested Batting Lineup:

1. Aaron
2. Joshua (catcher)
3. Miriam
4. Moses (clean-up)
5. Yocheved
6. Yitro
7. Tzipporah
8. Elijah
9. You

The Taskmasters:

Captain: Pharaoh

Suggested Batting Lineup:

1. Pharaoh
2. Abimelech (King of Gerar)
3. Sisera (Canaanite General)
4. Sennacherib (King of the Assyrians)
5. Nebuchadnezer (King of Babylonia)
6. Amalek (the evil leader of the tribe that attacked the back end of the Israelites during their wandering in the desert)
7. Goliath (a Philistine giant)
8. Haman (the bad guy in the Purim story)
9. Titus (the Roman leader during the destruction of the Second Temple in Jerusalem)

Coach's Tip: Ask your players to fill out a roster of a dream team of baseball players from any time in history and any league. Each player may fill out a roster with back up players, but should also keep a spot for him or herself. These players will help defeat Pharaoh's team of Taskmasters.

Your Lineup for Team Israelite:

Batter	Name of Player	Position
1.	______________________	______________
2.	______________________	______________
3.	______________________	______________
4.	______________________	______________
5.	______________________	______________
6.	______________________	______________
7.	______________________	______________
8.	______________________	______________
9.	______________________	**Designated hitter**
	______________________	**Pitcher**

Field Your Team with excellent players covering these positions: Pitcher, Catcher, 1st Base, 2nd Base, 3rd Base, Shortstop, Left Field, Center Field, Right Field

Let's Play Ball!

Announcer: Welcome to the Baseball Seder! A seder is a special meal or feast on the first night or two nights of Passover, in which we retell the story of the Jewish people and how they became free.

Announcer: Across the world, at the close of the 14th day of the Hebrew month of Nisan, Jewish people begin to celebrate Pesach, or Passover, and explain specific symbols (items that remind us of ideas or things that happened in the past). We use certain foods to help us tell the Passover story. When we taste the bitter herb, we feel the burning sadness of being a slave. Dipping vegetables into salt water helps us remember the tears of the slaves. The shank bone reminds us of a part of a sheep that used to be barbequed as a gift to God. The seder meal happens in a certain order (seder means "order" in Hebrew). We tell the story about how the Israelites once were slaves and then became free.

Announcer: Usually, we don't talk about baseball or sports during the Passover seder. It is a custom to ask "why is this night different from all other nights of the year." Tonight's seder is different because today is not a regular day, it is Passover (or we are preparing for Passover), and also because we are talking about baseball when we tell the story of the Jewish people and their journey from slavery to freedom thousands of years ago.

Announcer: Every spring, Jews celebrate the Passover seder and this festival of freedom. Baseball starts in the spring, too. This Haggadah that you are holding, the book that we use to tell the story of Passover, shows the Passover story as a baseball game (it's a long one with 15 innings). If you look hard enough, you might notice that the shank bone looks a little bit like a bat, and that matzah balls resemble baseballs. The Haggadah contains many songs with numbers in them. We have to count at the seder (4 questions, a story about 4 different kinds of children, 4 promises of taking the Israelites out of Egypt, 15 parts of the seder, 13 ways of describing God, 12 tribes of Israel, 1 baby goat). In baseball, we count numbers of strikes, balls, runs, errors, and averages. Even the positions the players have on the field are assigned certain numbers.

Announcer: To score in baseball, you have to arrive home. And in the story of the Exodus, when the Israelites finally arrive in the land of *Eretz Yisrael*, they are home, too. So, enough with this pre-game banter, ladies and gentlemen, boys and girls, let's get ready to start this game by singing a rousing version of "Take Me Out to the Seder."

"Take Me Out to the Seder"

(Sung to the tune of Jack Norworth and Albert Von Tilzer's 1908 classic baseball song, "Take Me Out to the Ballgame")

Take me out to the seder
Take me out to the crowds
Feed me some soup with a matzah ball
Pesach's in spring and is not in the fall
For we'll root, root, root for the Israelities
As they cross right through the Red Sea,
For it's one, two, three, four cups of wine
We rejoice that we are free.

Candle Lighting

Batter: Right before the sun sets as a Jewish festival or the Sabbath begins, it is a tradition to light candles and then recite blessings, as we welcome a special day.

Batter: You have to turn on the stadium lights in order to play the game. So let's bring some light into our seder. Play ball!

Adult Coach with a match lights the candles and recites:

Ba·ruch a·ta Adonai,	בָּרוּךְ אַתָּה יְיָ
E·lo·hei·nu me·lech ha·o·lam,	אֱלֹהֵינוּ מֶלֶךְ הָעוֹלָם,
a·sher kid·sha·nu b'mitz·vo·tav	אֲשֶׁר קִדְּשָׁנוּ בְּמִצְוֹתָיו,
v'tzi·va·nu l'had·lik	וְצִוָּנוּ לְהַדְלִיק
ner shel yom tov.	נֵר שֶׁל יוֹם טוֹב.

Blessed are You, Eternal our God, Ruler of the Universe, who has made our lives holy with the commandments and who has given us the religious responsibility of lighting the lights for the festivals.

Ba·ruch a·ta Adonai,	בָּרוּךְ אַתָּה יְיָ,
Eloheinu me·lech ha·o·lam,	אֱלֹהֵינוּ מֶלֶךְ הָעוֹלָם,
she·he·che·yanu v'ki·y'ma·nu	שֶׁהֶחֱיָנוּ וְקִיְּמָנוּ
v'hi·gi·ya·nu laz·man ha·zeh.	וְהִגִּיעָנוּ לַזְּמַן הַזֶּה.

Blessed are You, Eternal our God, Ruler of the Universe, who has kept us alive and brought us to this special time.

1st Inning: *Kadesh* (קַדֵּשׁ)
Festival Kiddush
First Cup of Wine/Grape Juice/Sports Drink

Batter: We are about to drink the first cup, which gives us energy to run around the bases and stay hydrated. Wine and grape juice are symbols of joy and happiness. Today, this drink reminds us of our dehydration in the desert of Sinai and how we were able to find water on our journey. Together, we raise this cup of celebration and energy and recite the proper blessing.

Over wine or grape juice:

Ba·ruch a·ta Adonai, Eloheinu
me·lech ha·o·lam, bo·rei p'ri ha·ga·fen.

בָּרוּךְ אַתָּה יְיָ, אֱלֹהֵינוּ
מֶלֶךְ הָעוֹלָם, בּוֹרֵא פְּרִי הַגָּפֶן.

Blessed are You, Eternal our God, Ruler of the universe, who creates the fruit of the vine.

Over a sports drink:

Ba·ruch a·ta Adonai, Eloheinu
me·lech ha·o·lam, she·ha·kol ni·h'yeh bid·va·ro.

בָּרוּךְ אַתָּה יְיָ, אֱלֹהֵינוּ
מֶלֶךְ הָעוֹלָם, שֶׁהַכֹּל נִהְיֶה בִּדְבָרוֹ.

Blessed are You, Eternal our God, Ruler of the universe, who creates all things according to the divine will.

Announcer: Well, ladies and gentlemen, boys and girls, it's time to drink your beverage while leaning and reclining to the left side. This is a way to show off that we are a free people who can relax like team owners. Let's do a wave motion with everyone at the table, taking turns standing up and raising up our hands.

2nd Inning: *Urchatz* (וּרְחַץ)
Washing the hands (no blessing recited)

Announcer: If your parents say it is okay, you may now *pretend* to spit in your hands the way professional baseball players do sometimes before taking the bat or grabbing the ball to pitch.

Batter: The high priests at the Temple in Jerusalem used to wash their hands in a special way to show respect for their important jobs and to God. We wash our hands for the first time in this seder in order to keep clean and show our respect for the ritual of eating.

3rd Inning: *Karpas* (כַּרְפַּס)
Dipping the greens or vegetable into saltwater

Batter: We are so happy that spring training has arrived, and that the season of Passover and baseball is upon us. The greens represent the flowers and trees that grow again each year. The baseball fields are bright green with life. We dip the parsley and other vegetables into saltwater. The water represents the tears of the Israelites who were slaves. It also could represent the tears of our team when we lose in the last inning and the sweat on our foreheads when we play in the hot sun.

Announcer: Please dip your green vegetable in the saltwater and recite this blessing.

Ba·ruch a·ta Adonai, Eloheinu
me·lech ha·o·lam, bo·rei p'ri ha·a·da·ma.

בָּרוּךְ אַתָּה יְיָ, אֱלֹהֵינוּ
מֶלֶךְ הָעוֹלָם, בּוֹרֵא פְּרִי הָאֲדָמָה.

Blessed are You, Eternal our God, Ruler of the Universe, who creates the fruits of the Earth.

Announcer: Although this does not happen too frequently at a baseball stadium where we eat lots of greasy foods, let's eat the greenery.

4th Inning: *Yachatz* (יַחַץ)

Breaking the Middle Matzah

Batter: Now we break the middle of these three matzahs (*matzot,* in Hebrew) into two pieces. The larger piece is set aside as the dessert matzah, or Afikoman. It will be hidden and retrieved like a great home run ball that has been hit into the stands. We can hold the matzah sideways like a baseball diamond and declare, "This is the bread of affliction that our ancestors ate in the land of Egypt. Let everyone who is hungry come and eat" at our concession stand. Now we celebrate this game here. Next year, we hope to celebrate at a ballpark in the Land of Israel. This year we are still like slaves in many ways. Next year, may we all be free agents.

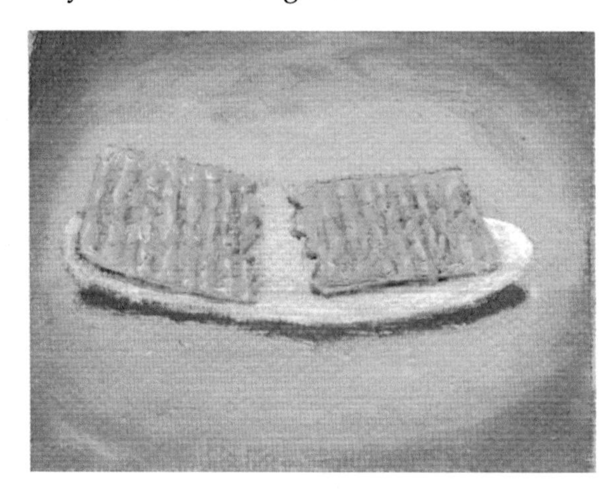

Coach's Tip: Now is the time to take the Afikoman pieces and distribute them to the children's labeled envelopes. At some point during the seder, you will need to leave the field and go out into the stands and hide those pieces of matzah without being detected. When the players retrieve the matzah (only upon your signal), you may give them small gifts or also elect to give a gift to a charitable organization of the team's choosing. (At this seder, gifts of baseball cards, chewing gum, team caps and gear are certainly appropriate.)

5th Inning: *Magid* (מַגִּיד)

The Story of Passover

Ha lach·ma an·ya di a·chalu av·ha·ta·na	הָא לַחְמָא עַנְיָא דִּי אֲכָלוּ אַבְהָתָנָא
b'ar·a d'Mitz·ra·yim.	בְּאַרְעָא דְמִצְרָיִם.
Kol dich·fin yei·tei v'yei·chol,	כָּל דִּכְפִין יֵיתֵי וְיֵכוֹל,
kol ditz·rich yei·tei v'yif·sach.	כָּל דִּצְרִיךְ יֵיתֵי וְיִפְסַח.
Ha·sha·ta ha·cha,	הָשַּׁתָּא הָכָא,
l'sha·na ha·ba·a b'ar·a d'Yis·ra·eil.	לְשָׁנָה הַבָּאָה בְּאַרְעָא דְיִשְׂרָאֵל.
Ha·sha·ta av·dei,	הָשַּׁתָּא עַבְדֵי,
l'sha·na ha·ba·a b'nei cho·rin.	לְשָׁנָה הַבָּאָה בְּנֵי חוֹרִין.

This is the bread of affliction which our ancestors ate in the land of Egypt. Let all who are hungry come and eat. Let all who are needy come and celebrate the Passover. Now we are here; next year may we be in Israel. Now we are slaves; next year may we be free people.

The Four Questions

Announcer: Well, friends, we've reached that favorite part of the seder when we start to tell the story of Passover. For those of us who haven't been to this combination of a ballgame and seder before, here's the lineup. The youngest child at the ballpark gets to sing these questions that introduce the seder. We spend the rest of the seder attempting to answer these questions. Freedom gives us the right to ask and answer questions.

מַה נִּשְׁתַּנָּה הַלַּיְלָה הַזֶּה
מִכָּל הַלֵּילוֹת?

Ma nish·ta·na ha·lai·la ha·zeh
mi·kol ha·lei·lot?

Why is this night different from all other nights?

שֶׁבְּכָל הַלֵּילוֹת אָנוּ אוֹכְלִין
חָמֵץ וּמַצָּה.
הַלַּיְלָה הַזֶּה כֻּלוֹ מַצָּה.

She·b'chol ha·lei·lot anu och·lin
cha·metz u·ma·tza,
ha·lai·la ha·zeh ku·lo ma·tza.

1. On all other nights we eat chametz and matzah.
Tonight, why do we eat only matzah?

שֶׁבְּכָל הַלֵּילוֹת אָנוּ אוֹכְלִין
שְׁאָר יְרָקוֹת.
הַלַּיְלָה הַזֶּה מָרוֹר.

She·b'chol ha·lei·lot a·nu och·lin
sh'ar y'ra·kot,
ha·lai·la ha·zeh ma·ror.

2. On all other nights we eat any kind of herbs.
Tonight, why do we eat bitter herbs?

שֶׁבְּכָל הַלֵּילוֹת אֵין אָנוּ
מַטְבִּילִין אֲפִילוּ פַּעַם אֶחָת.
הַלַּיְלָה הַזֶּה שְׁתֵּי פְעָמִים.

She·b'chol ha·lei·lot ein a·nu
mat·bi·lin a·fi·lu pa·am e·chat,
ha·lai·la ha·zeh sh'tei f'a·mim.

3. On all other nights we do not dip even once.
Tonight, why do we dip the greens twice?

שֶׁבְּכָל הַלֵּילוֹת אָנוּ אוֹכְלִין
בֵּין יוֹשְׁבִין וּבֵין מְסֻבִּין.
הַלַּיְלָה הַזֶּה כֻּלָּנוּ מְסֻבִּין.

She·b'chol ha·lei·lot a·nu och·lin
bein yosh·vin u·vein m'su·bin,
ha·lai·la ha·zeh ku·la·nu m'su·bin.

4. On all other nights we eat sitting or reclining.
Tonight, why do we all recline?

Avadim Hayinu עֲבָדִים הָיִינוּ

We Were Slaves

Announcer: As we uncover the plate piled with matzah, we recite these words and remember what our ancient relatives endured in Mitzrayim (the Hebrew word for Egypt). They were slaves and suffered, and because we are on their team, we experience their sadness, as well. When anyone is a slave, no one can truly be free.

עֲבָדִים הָיִינוּ לְפַרְעֹה בְּמִצְרָיִם. *(Avadim Hayinu l'Faroh b'Mitzrayim).* We were slaves to Pharaoh in Mitzrayim, but God brought us out with a strong hand and with an outstretched arm. Even if we all were wise scholars and sages, we would need to tell the story of the Exodus. Whoever expands upon the story is worthy of praise.

The Story of Rabbi Eliezer

Announcer: I have so many baseball tales to share with our audience. Rumor has it that Rabbi Eliezer, Rabbi Yehoshua, Rabbi Elazar ben Azaryah, Rabbi Akiva, and Rabbi Tarfon were old time baseball hall of famers who were so busy talking about the greatest baseball game ever against Pharaoh that they didn't notice that they had been talking and playing catch all night long. The teams they were coaching told them that it was already light outside and time to say morning prayers and warm up for the day's baseball games.

Announcer: Wow, that's quite a story. In the traditional Passover Haggadah, there's a story just like that about five old time rabbis with the exact same names you mentioned who were up talking about the Exodus from Egypt all night long at their seder. That's quite a coincidence. Maybe these rabbis were at the May 8, 1984 25-inning game between the Chicago White Sox and the Milwaukee Brewers? That game took eight hours and six minutes to play!

Announcer: The White Sox won 7-6, right?

Announcer: Yes, they did. But now we're at a seder, so we'd better get back to our favorite number of the night, the number four.

The Four Children

Batter: During our seder, we tell the story of four children who were trying to understand why Passover was important to their families. In the story, there is a wise child, a wicked one, one who is simple, and one who is so young that he or she doesn't know enough about religion to even ask any questions at all.

Batter: In baseball, there are four types of players. Legendary baseball manager, Tommy Lasorda, describes three main types of players: those who make it happen, those who watch it happen, and those who wonder what happens. The wise player asks about the meaning of all of the special rules of the game, even down to the most complicated details about the very rare "ground-rule triple award" (the penalty for blocking the path of a ball with a player's hat). Being wise means more than just being able to rattle off trivia.

Batter: The wicked baseball player asks: "why should you bother with the sacrifice fly when you are the one who is called out?" Because he is not interested in the team's success, we answer him in a tough way and suggest that he might not have merited being in the playoffs.

Batter: The simple baseball player says: "how did we manage to win this game?" We answer him by explaining that the team practiced a lot and followed the rules, and that our team had a great showing of strength.

Batter: Finally, we approach the baseball player who can't even speak a word by telling her that we did well at a game because that is just the way it was meant to be.

Announcer: Now it's time to tell the story of the Passover seder. See if you can mention everything that you see on the ads at the side of the next page:

Batter: The Torah explains that because of a famine in their land, when food would not grow, the Israelites traveled to Egypt, where Joseph, one of Jacob's sons was a powerful advisor to the Pharaoh. He had organized a way for the people of the Middle East not to starve during this time of little food.

Batter: But when a new Pharaoh, a new ruler, arose over Egypt, he decided not to remember what Joseph had done for the people. Fearing this group of foreigners and strangers living in his country, he decided to make the Jewish people slaves. Later, he ordered that all of the Jewish baby boys should be taken away.

Batter: Moses was a Jewish baby, whose mother and sister hid him so the Egyptians could not hurt him. They put him in a basket and floated him in the Nile River, where Pharaoh's daughter found him and adopted him. Moses' sister, Miriam, told the Pharaoh's daughter that she knew of a woman who could give milk to the baby and be his nanny. That was Yocheved, Moses' birth mother.

Batter: Moses grew up in the palace in Egypt as a prince. But, when he was older, he realized that the Jewish slaves were suffering terribly. Moses lost his temper one day when he witnessed Egyptian taskmasters hurting slaves. After getting into a fight with a taskmaster, Moses ran away from Egypt and ended up in the desert. There he saw a vision of a bush that was burning, but its leaves were perfectly green and not charred. Communicating with God in that special place, Moses was told to tell Pharaoh that he must let God's people go free.

Batter: Moses was not able to take the Jewish people out of Egypt and back to the Promised Land without help. Moses married a woman named Tzipporah, who gave him support. Her father, Yitro, shared wisdom with

Moses. Moses also relied on his sister, Miriam, for leadership, and his older brother, Aaron, to assist him when he approached Pharaoh. His helper, Joshua, also became a leader of the Jewish people. Moses and Aaron approached Pharaoh many times to ask him for mercy for the Jewish people and to let the Israelites go.

Batter: The Egyptians suffered from a series of horrible problems and sicknesses (plagues) until Pharaoh agreed to let the Israelites leave Egypt. Finally, the Israelites were granted their freedom and rushed to leave Egypt. But at the shores of the Sea of Reeds, which is sometimes called the Red Sea in this story, the Israelites were cornered by Pharaoh's chariots and armies. Pharaoh had changed his mind and decided that the Israelites must return to being slaves. A miracle occurred, and the Israelites passed through the sea. Miriam led the people in song and dance after the liberation.

Batter: While the Israelites wandered in the desert, they faced many challenges. Some of the Israelites wanted to pray to statues (especially a golden calf made out of melted jewelry). Moses went up a mountain twice to receive the Ten Commandments. The Israelites learned that being free meant that they had to follow rules, as well.

V'hi She'amdah (וְהִיא שֶׁעָמְדָה)

This is the Promise

Batter: We lift up our cups of wine or grape juice or sports drink. We recall that God kept the promise made to Abraham and Sarah, and to all Jews. In every generation, there are people who threaten to ruin the Jewish team's fun, but each time we defeat them with the help of God's strong arm and our working together as a unified team.

Announcer: וְהִיא שֶׁעָמְדָה לַאֲבוֹתֵינוּ וְלָנוּ. *(V'hi she'amda la'avoteinu v'lanu.)* And the Holy One, Blessed is God, saves us from our enemies' hands.

Announcer: Sorry to do this to all of our loyal fans, but we've been instructed to ask you to put down those drinks without taking a refreshing sip and to uncover the matzah at this time. We are remembering all of the teams throughout history that stood against us.

The Ten Plagues

Batter: In the Torah's Book of Exodus, we learn about ten horrible sicknesses and troubles that God sent to the Egyptians to convince Pharaoh to let the Israelites leave. Finally, after the last and most terrible plague, Pharaoh said he would free the slaves. But then he changed his mind and chased the Israelites with his army to the edge of the Sea of Reeds. The Egyptian army sank in the muddy waters after God threw a "sinker ball," and the Israelites escaped to safety on the other side of the sea.

Umpire: Pharaoh, you are out!

Batter: Although the seder is a time for joy, we take some sweetness out of our cups and remember the pain of the other team. When we win a game, we desire a victory that does not cause anyone else to be on a disabled list or get hurt for the rest of the season. To remember the suffering of others, we remove ten drops from our cups, one for each plague that the Egyptians experienced.

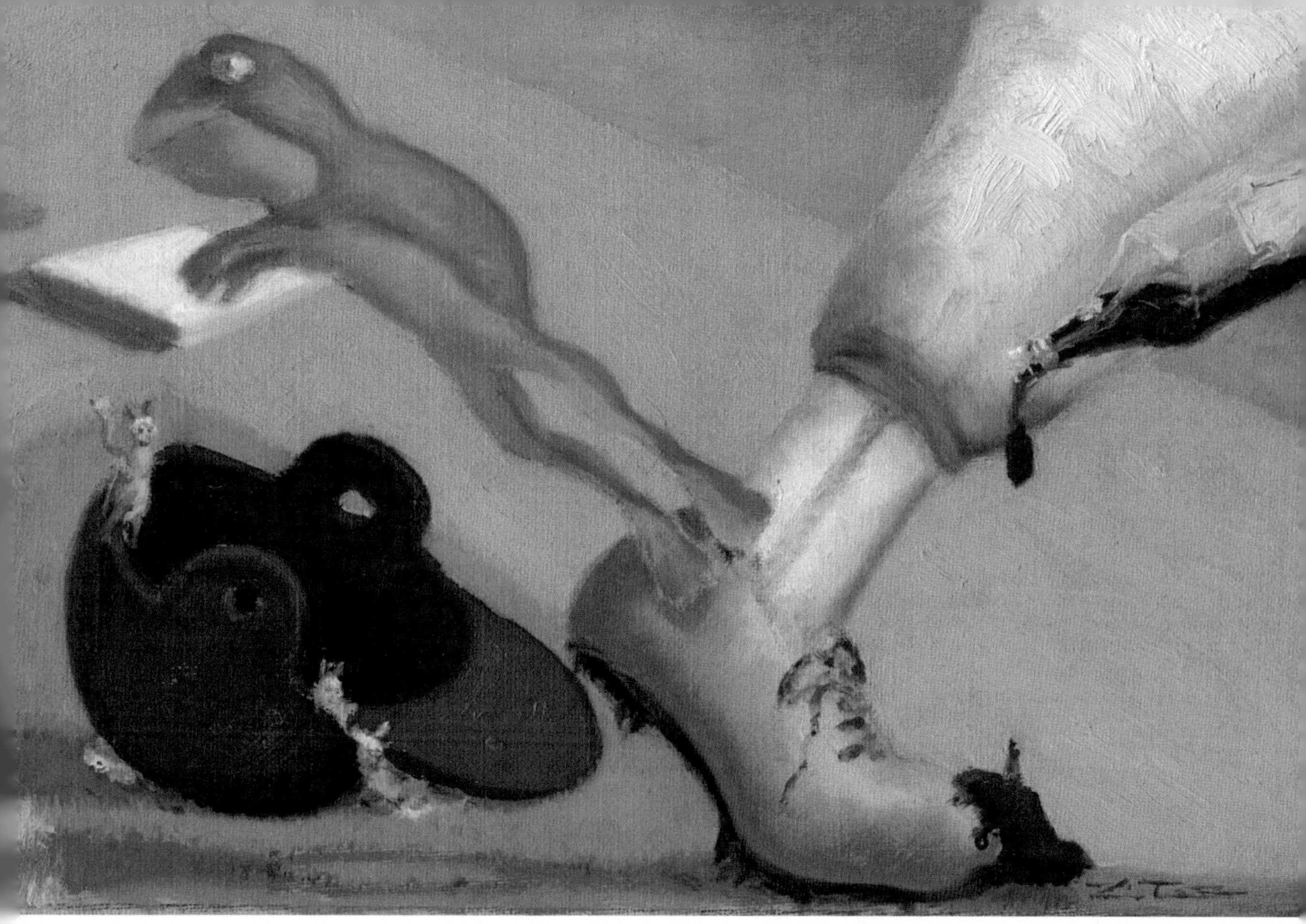

Batter: As each plague is recited in Hebrew and English, and the entire team repeats the name of the plague together, take a drop from your cup and place it on your plate with a spoon or your little finger.

Hebrew	Translation	Baseball Interpretation
Dam (דָּם)	Blood	Being hit with a baseball
Tz'fardei·a (צְפַרְדֵּעַ)	Frogs	Foul off of the foot
Kinim (כִּנִּים)	Lice	Lice in the helmet
Arov (עָרוֹב)	Wild Beasts	Wild animals on the field
Dever (דֶּבֶר)	Blight	Dead grass on the field
Sh'chin (שְׁחִין)	Boils	Blisters on the pitcher's fingers
Barad (בָּרָד)	Hail	Rainout
Arbeh (אַרְבֶּה)	Locusts	Swarming insects on the field
Choshech (חֹשֶׁךְ)	Darkness	Blackout of stadium lights
Makat B'chorot (מַכַּת בְּכוֹרוֹת)	Slaying of the First Born	Pitcher's nightmare/ line drive back to the pitcher

Dayenu (דַּיֵּנוּ)- It Would Have Been Enough

Batter: It would have been enough if the Israelites had just been set free from slavery in Egypt, but instead, God also gave us manna to eat in the desert, gave us the Sabbath, brought the Israelites to Mount Sinai, and helped us enter the land of Israel. For all of these gifts and so many more, we are grateful. "*Dayenu*" means, "it would have been enough for us." Passover is a time for us to appreciate our many blessings.

*I·lu ho·tzi·a·nu mi·Mitz·ra·ym, **da·yei·nu**!*	אִלּוּ הוֹצִיאָנוּ מִמִּצְרַיִם, דַּיֵּנוּ.
*I·lu na·tan la·nu et ha·Sha·bat, **da·yei·nu**!*	אִלּוּ נָתַן לָנוּ אֶת־הַשַּׁבָּת, דַּיֵּנוּ.
*I·lu na·tan la·nu et ha·To·ra, **da·yei·nu**!*	אִלּוּ נָתַן לָנוּ אֶת־הַתּוֹרָה, דַּיֵּנוּ.

Announcer: And here's a little baseball *Dayenu* to consider at this season.
It would have been enough if the Holy One allowed us to play baseball during the day, but we were also allowed to play at night.
It would have been enough if we were allowed to play at night and had not gotten a home run, but we were allowed to score in every inning.
It would have been enough if we were allowed to score in every inning,
but we were also allowed to win. *Dayenu*.

Explanation of the symbols of *Pesach* (פֶּסַח), *Matzah* (מַצָּה), and *Maror* (מָרוֹר)

Announcer: Rabbi Gamliel said that in order to tell the Passover story in the right way, we have to say the words *Pesach, Matzah,* and *Maror* and explain what they mean, even if we are having a seder all by ourselves and have to talk to ourselves.

Announcer: Sometimes I need to talk to myself in order to have an intelligent conversation. But now, let's figure out the meaning behind our team symbols of *Pesach, Matzah,* and *Maror*. I propose we also explain the meaning of the bat, the baseball diamond, and the chewing gum.

Batter: *Pesach* — the roasted shank bone is a symbol of the special sacrifice and barbeque that people gave to God at the Temple in Jerusalem. The Israelites said thank you to God for making sure that their homes were "passed over" during the unleashing of the plagues.

Batter: *Matzah* — the unleavened bread is a symbol of the speed at which the Israelites were forced to leave Egypt and escape from Pharaoh. There was no time to bake fluffy bread with yeast in it. Instead, the Israelites baked fast food matzah crackers for their trip.

Batter: *Maror* — the bitter herb represents the bitterness and pain of slavery. Jewish people should always be especially sensitive to others because we were once slaves in the land of Egypt. We can show sympathy for our fellow human beings and empathy (feelings of understanding because we also experienced something difficult).

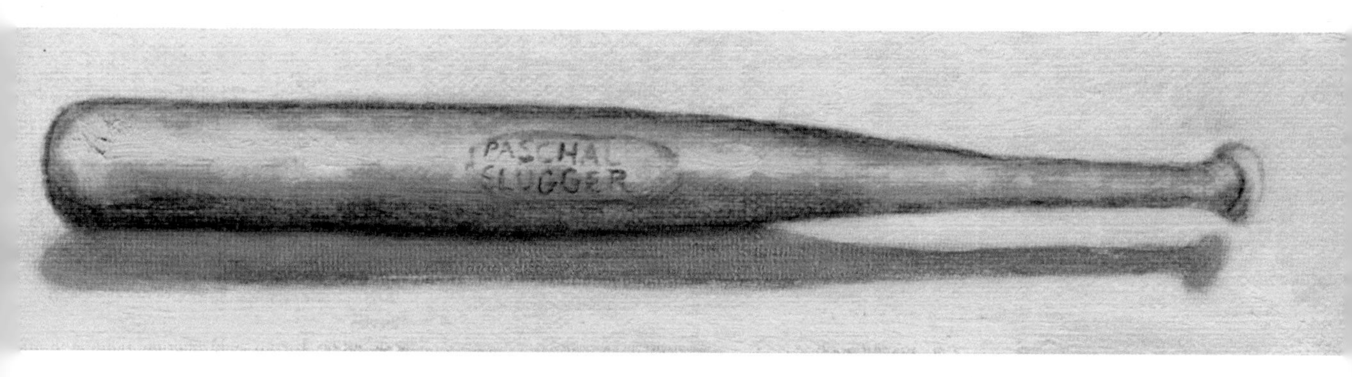

Announcer: Let's put in some new symbols for our baseball loving friends at home. As a former home run hitter, I think the bat is a great symbol for Passover.

The Bat — The bat symbolizes strength and power. It reminds us that it is important to be healthy and strong, but it is also crucial to use that strength in a disciplined and controlled way. Swinging a bat around wildly does not result in effective hitting. You have to watch and know what kind of swing is just right for the pitch. It is important to have inner, emotional strength.

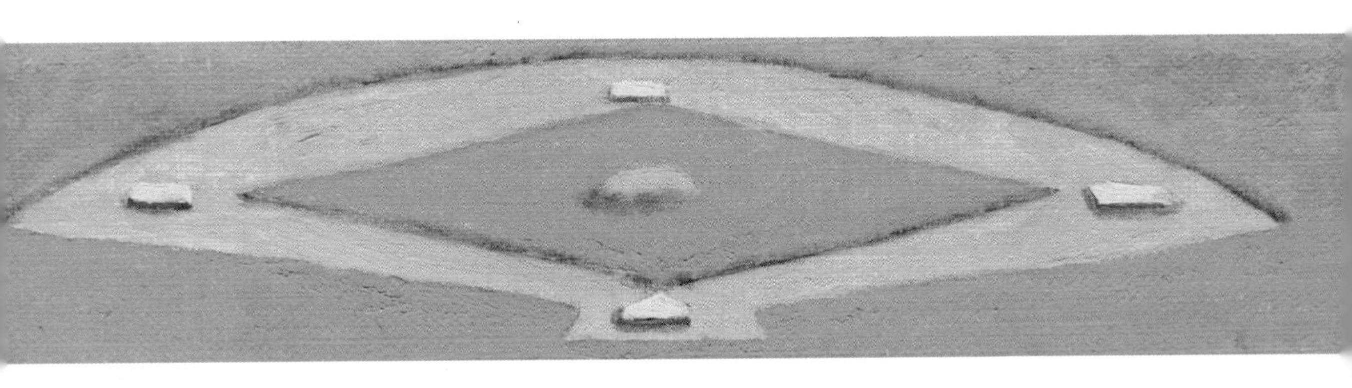

The Baseball Diamond — The baseball diamond symbolizes the fields of springtime. Coincidentally, if you draw a line down the middle of the diamond you have designed half of a Jewish star. In life, we can't just skip around from one place to another. Sometimes you have to go through steps to get to the desired goal, base by base. You have to show patience, and you can't always run to the next base if the runner in front of you does not advance. You have to be aware of what is going on around you in baseball and in life, or you will be called out.

Announcer: Here's another symbol that is pretty sweet!

The Chewing Gum — Many baseball players chew gum during the game. The chewing gum represents the actions of our mouths. What we say is very important. Words of kindness, helpfulness, and encouragement make our team stronger. When we make fun of teammates' mistakes and hurt feelings with our words, we use our mouths in a negative way. Not too many years ago, many baseball players chewed on a plant called tobacco that caused them to get diseases. When they realized they were hurting themselves, they changed their habits. We can learn to take the bitterness out of our mouths, as well.

B'chol Dor Vador (בְּכָל־דּוֹר וָדוֹר)

In Every Generation

Batter: In every generation, we should try to imagine that we left Egypt. The Torah says that you should tell your children how *you* were set free from Egypt, even though it happened thousands of years ago.

Batter: At this seder, we imagine that we are playing a baseball game and are trying to make it home to the Land of Israel. It is almost as though we were playing on Egyptian fields and running those bases. Pharaoh was trying to hit us with a baseball. But we had the stronger team and the most faith, and so we prevailed.

B'tzeit Yis·ra·eil mi·Mitz·ra·yim,	בְּצֵאת יִשְׂרָאֵל מִמִּצְרָיִם,
beit Ya·akov mei·am lo·ez.	בֵּית יַעֲקֹב מֵעַם לֹעֵז.
Ha·y'ta Y'hu·da l'kod·sho,	הָיְתָה יְהוּדָה לְקָדְשׁוֹ,
Yis·ra·eil mam·sh'lo·tav.	יִשְׂרָאֵל מַמְשְׁלוֹתָיו.
Ha·yam ra·a va·ya·nos,	הַיָּם רָאָה וַיָּנֹס,
ha·yar·dein yi·sov l'a·chor.	הַיַּרְדֵּן יִסֹּב לְאָחוֹר.

When Israel made its Exodus from Egypt, the House of Jacob from a foreign place, Judah became God's special place, Israel became God's dominion. *from Psalm 114*

Second Cup of Wine/Grape Juice/Sports Drink

Batter: Now that the story of our liberation has been retold, we can finally drink our second cup of wine or grape juice or sports drink. We say the special blessings once again together.

Over wine or grape juice:

Ba·ruch a·ta Adonai, Eloheinu
me·lech ha·o·lam, bo·rei p'ri ha·ga·fen.

בָּרוּךְ אַתָּה יְיָ, אֱלֹהֵינוּ
מֶלֶךְ הָעוֹלָם, בּוֹרֵא פְּרִי הַגָּפֶן.

Blessed are You, Eternal our God, Ruler of the universe, who creates the fruit of the vine.

Over a sports drink:

Ba·ruch a·ta Adonai, Eloheinu
me·lech ha·o·lam, she·ha·kol ni·h'yeh bid·va·ro.

בָּרוּךְ אַתָּה יְיָ, אֱלֹהֵינוּ
מֶלֶךְ הָעוֹלָם, שֶׁהַכֹּל נִהְיֶה בִּדְבָרוֹ.

Blessed are You, Eternal our God, Ruler of the universe, who creates all things according to the divine will.

Announcer: Drink your beverage while leaning and reclining to the left side. Do a "wave" with everyone at the table, taking turns standing up and raising up your hands. In the words of the great Chicago Cubs Hall of Famer, Ernie Banks, "It's a great day for a ballgame; let's play two." It's a great day for a seder, let's enjoy this second cup!

6th Inning: Rachtzah (רָחְצָה)

Washing Your Hands

Batter: Now, it's time to wash our hands as we prepare to eat our meal. The high priests at the holy Temple in Jerusalem used to wash their hands before they would pray in their special way. We wash our hands to keep healthy, too. We recite this special blessing together. Take a "pitcher" of water and wash those hands without your baseball gloves on.

Ba·ruch a·ta Adonai Eloheinu me·lech	בָּרוּךְ אַתָּה יְיָ אֱלֹהֵינוּ מֶלֶךְ
ha·o·lam, a·sher kid·sha·nu b'mitz·vo·tav	הָעוֹלָם, אֲשֶׁר קִדְּשָׁנוּ בְּמִצְוֹתָיו,
v'tzi·va·nu al n'ti·lat ya·da·yim.	וְצִוָּנוּ עַל נְטִילַת יָדָיִם.

Blessed are You, Eternal our God, Ruler of the Universe, who has made our lives holy with the commandments and who has given us the religious responsibility of lifting up our hands (for washing).

Seventh Inning Stretch

Announcer: All right, fans, before you run off to get your meal, let's take a moment to stretch those legs and sing "Take Me Out to the Seder" one more time!

"Take Me Out to the Seder"

Take me out to the seder
Take me out to the crowds
Feed me some soup with a matzah ball
Pesach's in spring and is not in the fall
For we'll root, root, root for the Israelities
As they cross right through the Red Sea,
For it's one, two, three, four cups of wine
We rejoice that we are free.

7th Inning: Motzi (מוֹצִיא)

Blessing Over the Food

Announcer: Now, we can recite the blessings for the matzah and eat a piece from the top deck of the seder plate.

Ba·ruch a·ta Adonai,	בָּרוּךְ אַתָּה יְיָ,
Eloheinu me·lech ha·o·lam,	אֱלֹהֵינוּ מֶלֶךְ הָעוֹלָם,
ha·mo·tzi le·chem min ha·a·retz.	הַמּוֹצִיא לֶחֶם מִן הָאָרֶץ.

Blessed are You, Eternal our God, Ruler of the universe, who brings forth bread from the earth.

8th Inning: Matzah (מַצָּה)

Blessing Over the Matzah

Ba·ruch a·ta Adonai Eloheinu me·lech	בָּרוּךְ אַתָּה יְיָ אֱלֹהֵינוּ מֶלֶךְ
ha·o·lam, a·sher kid·sha·nu b'mitz·vo·tav	הָעוֹלָם, אֲשֶׁר קִדְּשָׁנוּ בְּמִצְוֹתָיו,
v'tzi·va·nu al a·chi·lat ma·tza.	וְצִוָּנוּ עַל אֲכִילַת מַצָּה.

Blessed are You, Eternal our God, Ruler of the Universe, who has made our lives holy with the commandments and has given us the religious responsibility of eating matzah.

9th Inning: Maror (מָרוֹר)

Blessing Over the Bitter Herb

Batter: We dip the bitter herb into the sweet charoset and recite the special blessing. There's no leaning or resting on the bench now, because we remember how hard and difficult it was to be a slave.

Ba·ruch a·ta Adonai Eloheinu me·lech	בָּרוּךְ אַתָּה יְיָ אֱלֹהֵינוּ מֶלֶךְ
ha·o·lam, a·sher kid·sha·nu b'mitz·vo·tav	הָעוֹלָם, אֲשֶׁר קִדְּשָׁנוּ בְּמִצְוֹתָיו
v'tzi·va·nu al a·chi·lat ma·ror.	וְצִוָּנוּ עַל אֲכִילַת מָרוֹר.

Blessed are You, Eternal our God, Ruler of the Universe, who has made our lives holy with the commandments and has given us the religious responsibility of eating the bitter herbs.

EXTRA INNINGS! 10th Inning: Korech (כּוֹרֵךְ)

The Hillel Sandwich

Batter: Rabbi Hillel was a leader and scholar who was famous for his brilliance and his compassion. Baseball players should not just be skilled technicians. They need heart, too. In the Torah's Book of Numbers, we are told that we should eat matzah and bitter herbs together. Hillel made a sandwich with the matzah and the herbs. We put charoset on it, too, for a little added sweetness.

> **Coach's Tip:** Combine matzah, bitter herb or horseradish, and charoset — (the apple/walnut mixture) to make a sandwich just like Rabbi Hillel did.

11th Inning: Shulchan Orech (שֻׁלְחָן עוֹרֵךְ)

Festive Meal

Announcer: It's time to go to the concession stands and get a delicious meal to eat during the game. You can put aside the Haggadah in a safe place, and enjoy your holiday meal with your dining room table manners and not your ballpark ones.

12th Inning: Tzafun (צָפוּן)

Search and Recovery of the Afikoman

Announcer: A home run has been hit into the stands. Your job is to recover that ball. Go look for the envelope with your name on it with your piece of the dessert matzah, the Afikoman. The seder cannot be completed until you have found that special piece of the matzah, which will be ransomed with a reward. Share the matzah you find with everyone at your seder.

Batter: Here are the pieces of the Afikoman, which we will now eat, as we complete this seder. These pieces of cracker remind us of a special lamb that was eaten at the end of the seder in olden times.

Batter: We do not keep the Afikoman in a clear box as a trophy to remember this night. Sharing this matzah, we remember that we live in a special time and place in history where we have much freedom and physical comforts. Life was not always easy for many Jewish people. And life remains difficult for many people all across the world.

Batter: Let these crumbs of matzah encourage us to fix the broken pieces of our world, to help those people who worry about having enough food or a safe place to live and go to school. Let us put these broken pieces together.

13th Inning: Barech (בָּרֵךְ) Blessing After the Meal

Announcer: Okay, folks. We've eaten this delicious meal. It's time for an enthusiastic ovation for the real head of this team, none other than the Creator of the Universe. Let's give a cheer to God with the *Birkat Ha-Mazon,* the Grace After the Meal.

Ba·ruch a·ta Adonai, Eloheinu me·lech ha·o·lam,
ha·zan et ha·o·lam ku·lo b'tu·vo b'chein
b'che·sed u·v'ra·cha·mim. Hu no·tein le·chem
l'chol ba·sar ki l'o·lam chas·do.
U·v'tu·vo ha·ga·dol ta·mid lo cha·sar la·nu
v'al yech·sar la·nu ma·zon l'o·lam va·ed.
Ba·a·vur sh'mo ha·ga·dol,
ki hu Eil zan u·m'far·neis la·kol
u·mei·tiv la·kol u·mei·chin ma·zon
l'chol bri·o·tav a·sher ba·ra.
Ba·ruch a·ta Adonai, ha·zan et ha·kol.

בָּרוּךְ אַתָּה יְיָ, אֱלֹהֵינוּ מֶלֶךְ הָעוֹלָם,
הַזָּן אֶת הָעוֹלָם כֻּלּוֹ בְּטוּבוֹ בְּחֵן
בְּחֶסֶד וּבְרַחֲמִים. הוּא נוֹתֵן לֶחֶם
לְכָל בָּשָׂר כִּי לְעוֹלָם חַסְדּוֹ.
וּבְטוּבוֹ הַגָּדוֹל תָּמִיד לֹא חָסַר לָנוּ,
וְאַל יֶחְסַר לָנוּ מָזוֹן לְעוֹלָם וָעֶד.
בַּעֲבוּר שְׁמוֹ הַגָּדוֹל,
כִּי הוּא אֵל זָן וּמְפַרְנֵס לַכֹּל
וּמֵטִיב לַכֹּל, וּמֵכִין מָזוֹן
לְכֹל בְּרִיּוֹתָיו אֲשֶׁר בָּרָא.
בָּרוּךְ אַתָּה יְיָ, הַזָּן אֶת הַכֹּל.

Blessed are You, Eternal our God, who sustains the whole world with goodness, kindness and mercy. God gives food to all creatures, for God's mercy is everlasting. Through God's abundance, we have never yet been in want; may we never be in want of sustenance. God sustains all, is kind to all, and provides food for all the creatures of the world. Blessed are You, Eternal our God, who provides food for all.

O·seh sha·lom bim·ro·mav,	עֹשֶׂה שָׁלוֹם בִּמְרוֹמָיו,
hu ya·a·seh sha·lom, a·lei·nu	הוּא יַעֲשֶׂה שָׁלוֹם, עָלֵינוּ
v'al kol Yis·ra·eil v'im·ru: A·men.	וְעַל כָּל יִשְׂרָאֵל, וְאִמְרוּ אָמֵן.

May the One who makes peace in the heavens create peace over us and over all Israel. And let us say, Amen.

Third Cup of Wine/Grape Juice/Sports Drink

Batter: Just as we enjoyed two other glasses of wine or grape juice or sports drinks earlier in the seder, we take another sip out of our beautiful cups. In thanks to God for creating us and bringing us to this festive day in freedom, we lift our glasses high and sing.

Over wine or grape juice:

Ba·ruch a·ta Adonai, Eloheinu	בָּרוּךְ אַתָּה יְיָ, אֱלֹהֵינוּ
me·lech ha·o·lam, bo·rei p'ri ha·ga·fen.	מֶלֶךְ הָעוֹלָם, בּוֹרֵא פְּרִי הַגָּפֶן.

Blessed are You, Eternal our God, Ruler of the universe, who creates the fruit of the vine.

Over a sports drink:

Ba·ruch a·ta Adonai, Eloheinu	בָּרוּךְ אַתָּה יְיָ, אֱלֹהֵינוּ
me·lech ha·o·lam, she·ha·kol ni·h'yeh bid·va·ro.	מֶלֶךְ הָעוֹלָם, שֶׁהַכֹּל נִהְיֶה בִּדְבָרוֹ.

Blessed are You, Eternal our God, Ruler of the universe, who creates all things according to the divine will.

Coach's Tip: Drink your beverage while leaning and reclining to the left side. Do a wave motion with everyone at the table, taking turns standing up and raising up your hands.

Elijah's and Miriam's Cups

Announcer: It is the time of our seder when we tip our hats to that brave veteran, the prophet, Elijah. He reminds us that if we all try to be kind and helpful, then peace can come to the world. An old story tells us that Elijah went to heaven in a chariot made out of fire. Let us strive to be like Elijah and bring fire and passion to our game and our lives. Let us try to work hard at everything we do. Carefully, let's pour a bit of our own drink into a beautiful goblet for Elijah. If we work together, we can bring about a time of harmony and joy.

Announcer: In baseball, we are usually talking about boy players and coaches. But did you know that there was a women's league of baseball during the time of World War II? It was called the All-American Girls Professional Baseball League. Both boys and girls can show great talent at baseball. At our seder, Miriam's Cup sits at our table, too, as a way to honor one of the heroines of the Passover story. When Miriam was a little girl, she saved Moses and helped him navigate his floating basket in the Nile River. She led dancing at the shores of the Sea when the Israelites were rescued from Pharaoh. Legend teaches that wherever Miriam went in the desert, a well of pure, refreshing water would spring up. Let us strive to be like Miriam, so that wherever we go we make the world a better place filled with music and gratitude and life giving hope.

> **Coach's Tip:** The children go to the door and welcome in Elijah and Miriam while we sing.

Ei·li·ya·hu ha·na·vi,	אֵלִיָּהוּ הַנָּבִיא,
Ei·li·ya·hu ha·tish·bi;	אֵלִיָּהוּ הַתִּשְׁבִּי;
Ei·li·ya·hu, Ei·li·ya·hu,	אֵלִיָּהוּ, אֵלִיָּהוּ,
Ei·li·ya·hu ha·gil·a·di.	אֵלִיָּהוּ הַגִּלְעָדִי.
Bim·hei·ra v'ya·mei·nu, ya·vo ei·lei·nu;	בִּמְהֵרָה בְיָמֵינוּ, יָבֹא אֵלֵינוּ;
im Ma·shi·ach ben Da·vid,	עִם מָשִׁיחַ בֶּן דָּוִד,
im Ma·shi·ach ben Da·vid.	עִם מָשִׁיחַ בֶּן דָּוִד.

14th Inning: Hallel (הַלֵּל)

Hymns of Praise

Announcer: We fill our fourth cup and sing these favorite songs praising the God of our home team.

Ho·du l'Adonai ki tov,	הודוּ לַיְי כִּי טוֹב,
Ki l'o·lam chas·do.	כִּי לְעוֹלָם חַסְדּוֹ.
L'o·seh nif·la·ot g'do·lot l'va·do.	לְעֹשֵׂה נִפְלָאוֹת גְּדֹלוֹת לְבַדּוֹ,
Ki l'o·lam chas·do.	כִּי לְעוֹלָם חַסְדּוֹ.

Give thanks to God, for God is good, God's kindness endures forever;
To God who alone does great wonders, God's kindness endures forever.

from Psalm 136

Innings	1	2	3	4	5	6	7	8	9	10	11	12	13	14	15	Runs
Israelites	0	0	0	0	10	0	0	0	0	0	0	0	0	0	1	11
Taskmasters	10	0	0	0	0	0	0	0	0	0	0	0	0	0	0	10

Fourth Cup of Wine/Grape Juice/Sports Drink

Batter: The fourth and final cup celebrates God's promise to take us out of slavery to be a special people for God. We are holy and special when we treat each other and our world in a way filled with integrity and honor. A team may brag about having the best players in the world, but they don't always win unless they work together and have respect for each other. This cup reminds us to work together. Let us raise our glasses and sing this blessing one more time.

Over wine or grape juice:

Ba·ruch a·ta Adonai, Eloheinu
me·lech ha·o·lam, bo·rei p'ri ha·ga·fen.

בָּרוּךְ אַתָּה יְיָ, אֱלֹהֵינוּ
מֶלֶךְ הָעוֹלָם, בּוֹרֵא פְּרִי הַגָּפֶן.

Blessed are You, Eternal our God, Ruler of the universe, who creates the fruit of the vine.

Over a sports drink:

Ba·ruch a·ta Adonai, Eloheinu
me·lech ha·o·lam, she·ha·kol ni·h'yeh bid·va·ro.

בָּרוּךְ אַתָּה יְיָ, אֱלֹהֵינוּ
מֶלֶךְ הָעוֹלָם, שֶׁהַכֹּל נִהְיֶה בִּדְבָרוֹ.

Blessed are You, Eternal our God, Ruler of the universe, who creates all things according to the divine will.

Announcer: Drink your beverage while leaning and reclining to the left side.

> **Coach's Tip:** Do a wave motion with everyone at the table, taking turns standing up and raising up your hands.

Batter: Moses and Aaron and Miriam get a lot of publicity on Passover. I like the brave guy, Nachshon, who was the first person to walk into the Sea of Reeds. Sometimes, you have to be bold and have a lot of faith.

Batter: Jackie Robinson was like Nachshon in the world of baseball. When he started playing for the Brooklyn Dodgers in April of 1947, he was the first African American to play outside of the Negro Leagues. At a time in American history when African Americans were not treated equally, Jackie Robinson's incredible skill, character, and bravery helped Americans move forward to grant civil rights to all citizens, no matter what color they were. Number 42 made a huge difference with his bat and his heart.

S'firat HaOmer (סְפִירַת הָעֹמֶר)
Counting the Omer Starting on the 2nd Night of Passover

Batter: Every year, I count down from Spring Training to Opening Day. I can't wait until we throw out the first baseball of the season!

Announcer: On the second night of Passover, it is a tradition to start counting the seven weeks up to the Festival of Shavuot. We celebrate our freedom from slavery at Passover and rejoice in the giving of the Torah on Shavuot. Each day is filled with meaning. We show honor for this tradition and stand up, as we count the days in between these holidays.

Ba·ruch a·ta Adonai	בָּרוּךְ אַתָּה יְיָ
Eloheinu me·lech ha·o·lam,	אֱלֹהֵינוּ מֶלֶךְ הָעוֹלָם,
a·sher kid·sha·nu b'mitz·vo·tav	אֲשֶׁר קִדְּשָׁנוּ בְּמִצְוֹתָיו,
v'tzi·va·nu al s'fi·rat ha·o·mer.	וְצִוָּנוּ עַל סְפִירַת הָעֹמֶר.

Blessed are You, Eternal our God, Ruler of the Universe, who has made our lives holy with the commandments and who has given us the religious responsibility of counting the Omer.

Ha·yom yom e·chad la·o·mer.	הַיּוֹם יוֹם אֶחָד לָעֹמֶר.

Today is the first day of the Omer.

15th Inning: Nirtzah (נִרְצָה)

Conclusion

Seder Recap

Announcer: Now our seder is completed. It's been a long, but exciting game. We've watched incredible base running. The Israelites started out at home plate, up at bat, in the land of Canaan, with Abraham and Sarah, the first Jews.

Announcer: Then, they made it to first base, the land of Egypt. They had a dangerous experience there, with a strong left-handed first baseman on the Pharaoh's team.

Announcer: Finally, the Israelites made it to second base, representing the 430 years of slavery under the cruel taskmasters. The Israelites suffered and were far away from their home in Israel.

Announcer: Third base stands for the time of the Exodus, when the Israelites became free. They wandered in the Wilderness of Sinai for 40 years. It was hot and perilous and filled with scorpions and cruel Amalekite tribes who attacked and picked on the rookies and the oldest members of thc team.

Announcer: Home base is the Promised Land of Israel. Before arriving home, the Israelites received the Torah and pledged to be a holy and good nation. They had some troubles getting through the catcher to home, but they slid home with faith and skill. The story of the Exodus is not the story of a home run on a beautiful, spring day. It is a long, hard fought trip through each and every base. But most of the players end up at home in the Promised Land.

Batter: On Passover, we remember the miracles that surround us every day. In a traditional Haggadah, there are stories of God's miracles taking place at the mysterious hour of midnight. It came to pass at midnight that God saved Abraham and Sarah, Jacob, and Daniel. Light up the darkness as the light of day!

Batter: In Fairbanks, Alaska, 160 miles south of the Arctic Circle, God lights up the darkness on the first day of summer each year. It's light for almost the entire day of the summer solstice. At the Midnight Sun Game, the Alaska Goldpanners host a baseball game in all natural light. The first pitch starts at 10:30 PM, and the games always go past midnight. This baseball game came to pass at midnight.

The Entire Team:

Va·y'hi ba·cha·tzi ha·lai·la וַיְהִי בַּחֲצִי הַלַּיְלָה

And it came to pass at midnight.

Batter: We have explained the special symbols at our table, and we have celebrated the freedom of the Jewish people. We are grateful for the privilege of living in a land of democracy and freedom. This seder helps remind us that we must work together to help everyone experience freedom. Even if our team loses game after game, there is always the hope that next year, we will win the World Series!

Batter: On the last day of Passover, Jewish people in synagogue chant verses from the Bible from the Book of Isaiah. This prophet explains that one day everyone will be treated with justice and fairness. Peace will take over the world, and even rivals will be kind to one another. Lions and lambs will live together in safety. Maybe even Yankees and Red Sox fans will make peace, and a "signal will be held up," and everyone in the field will be called home and will be able to run the bases safely. There will be peace and singing and the drawing up of water from the fountains of triumph.

The Entire Team:

L'sha·na ha·ba·a bi·ru·sha·la·yim! לְשָׁנָה הַבָּאָה בִּירוּשָׁלָיִם

Next year in Jerusalem!

Joyful Songs of Counting

Announcer: Before everyone leaves the stadium, let's sing some old favorites from Passover seders. Now, "Who Knows One?"

Announcer: Sure I know who won! The Israelites won this game.

Announcer: No, no. I said, "Who Knows One," that Passover song that tells about one God; two tablets for the Ten Commandments; the three patriarchs (Abraham, Isaac, and Jacob); four matriarchs (Sarah, Rebecca, Rachel, and Leah); five books of the Torah; six orders of the Mishnah; seven days of the week; eight days leading to a bris or baby naming; nine months leading to having a baby; ten commandments; eleven stars in Joseph's dream; twelve tribes of Israel; and thirteen attributes of God.

Announcer: I know this baseball version of "Who Knows One." Let's sing it now.

Who Knows One? (A Baseball Version of "*Echad Mi Yodeah?*" Rap)

Who knows One? I know One. One is the World Series,
One is the World Series, One is the World Series in the heaven and the earth.
Ooh, ahh, ooh, ooh, ooh, ahh.

Who knows Two? I know Two. Two are the teams of the game. (Clap, clap)
And One is the World Series, One is the World Series,
One is the World Series in the heaven and the earth. Ooh, ahh, ooh, ooh, ooh, ahh.

Who knows Three? I know Three. Three are the outs of the inning.
And Two are the teams of the game. (Clap, clap)
And One is the World Series, One is the World Series,
One is the World Series in the heaven and the earth. Ooh, ahh, ooh, ooh, ooh, ahh.

Who knows Four? I know Four. Four is the number of the bases.
Three are the outs of the inning.
And Two are the teams of the game. (Clap, clap)
And One is the World Series, One is the World Series,
One is the World Series in the heaven and the earth. Ooh, ahh, ooh, ooh, ooh, ahh.

Who knows Five? I know Five. Five is the number Hank Greenberg wore.
Four is the number of the bases. Three are the outs of the inning.
And Two are the teams of the game. (Clap, clap)
And One is the World Series, One is the World Series,
One is the World Series in the heaven and the earth. Ooh, ahh, ooh, ooh, ooh, ahh.

Who knows Six? I know Six. Six is the code for the shortstop.
Five is the number Hank Greenberg wore.
Four is the number of the bases. Three are the outs of the inning.
And Two are the teams of the game. (Clap, clap)
And One is the World Series, One is the World Series,
One is the World Series in the heaven and the earth. Ooh, ahh, ooh, ooh, ooh, ahh.

Who knows Seven? I know Seven. Seven is the inning when we do the stretch.
Six is the code for the shortstop. Five is the number Hank Greenberg wore.
Four is the number of the bases. Three are the outs of the inning.
And Two are the teams of the game. (Clap, clap)
And One is the World Series, One is the World Series,
One is the World Series in the heaven and the earth. Ooh, ahh, ooh, ooh, ooh, ahh.

Who knows Eight? I know Eight.
Eight was the perfect game in history that Koufax pitched.
Seven is the inning when we do the stretch.
Six is the code for the shortstop. Five is the number Hank Greenberg wore.
Four is the number of the bases. Three are the outs of the inning.
And Two are the teams of the game. (Clap, clap)
And One is the World Series, One is the World Series,
One is the World Series in the heaven and the earth. Ooh, ahh, ooh, ooh, ooh, ahh.

Who knows Nine? I know Nine. Nine are the players in a baseball game.
Eight was the perfect game in history that Koufax pitched.
Seven is the inning when we do the stretch.
Six is the code for the shortstop. Five is the number Hank Greenberg wore.
Four is the number of the bases. Three are the outs of the inning.
And Two are the teams of the game. (Clap, clap)
And One is the World Series, One is the World Series,
One is the World Series in the heaven and the earth. Ooh, ahh, ooh, ooh, ooh, ahh.

Announcer: Now, for one more encore, let's sing about a baseball card, my father bought as a gift for the seder.

Announcer: We used to sing about a baby goat that my father bought for seder. There was a dog, a cat, a stick, some water, even an angel in that song.

Announcer: Let's try "A Baseball Card" to the tune of "*Chad Gadya,*" showing how everything on earth is connected. Then, we can sing "*Adir Hu*" praising God and asking for the Creator of the Universe to build a stadium of peace.

A Baseball Card (A Baseball Version of "*Chad Gadya*")

A baseball card, a baseball card,
My father bought as an Afikoman present for the seder.
Baseball card, Baseball card.

Then came the ball that bounced right off my card,
My father bought as a gift for the seder.
Baseball card, Baseball card.

Then came the bat that hit, hit, hit the ball
that touched my card he bought for the seder.
Baseball Card, Baseball Card.

Then came the gloves that grabbed, grabbed, grabbed the bat
that hit the ball, that touched my card he bought for the seder.
Baseball Card, Baseball Card.

Then came the mitt that hid, hid, hid the gloves
that grabbed the bat, that hit the ball, that touched my card he bought for the seder.
Baseball Card, Baseball Card.

Then came the cap that covered up the mitt
that hid the gloves, that grabbed the bat, that hit the ball
that touched my card he bought for the seder.
Baseball Card, Baseball Card.

Then came the cleats that dirtied up the cap
that covered up the mitt, that hid the gloves, that grabbed the bat, that hit the ball
that touched my card he bought for the seder.
Baseball Card, Baseball Card.

Then came the helmet that knocked over my cleats
that dirtied up the cap, that covered up the mitt, that hid the gloves,
that grabbed the bat, that hit the ball, that touched my card he bought for the seder.
Baseball Card, Baseball Card.

Then came the heart guard, blessed be the padding,
that was important like the helmet, that knocked over my cleats,
that dirtied up the cap, that covered up the mitt, that hid the gloves,
that grabbed the bat, that hit the ball, that touched my card he bought for the seder.
Baseball Card, Baseball Card.

Batter: If you liked that song, we could all chime in with "*Chad Gadya,*" "An Only Kid." And the "kid" we are singing about is not "The Kid" Gary Carter, who was a catcher and baseball hall of famer who helped the Mets win the World Series in 1986. In English or Aramaic (a language closely related to Hebrew), this tune adds up to a lot of fun. Don't worry. After being chased by cats, dogs, sticks, and fire, the underdog (or undergoat in this case) wins big!

Then came the Holy One Blessed be God
who slew the Angel of Death
that killed the butcher
that slaughtered the ox
that drank the water
that quenched the fire
that burned the stick
that beat the dog
that bit the cat
that ate the kid
my father bought for two *zuzim;*
chad gadya, chad gadya.

Adir Hu אַדִּיר הוּא
God is Mighty

A·dir Hu, yiv·neh vei·to b'ka·rov,
bim·hei·ra, bim·hei·ra, b'ya·mei·nu b'ka·rov.
Eil b'nei, b'nei veit·cha b'ka·rov.

אַדִּיר הוּא, יִבְנֶה בֵיתוֹ בְּקָרוֹב,
בִּמְהֵרָה בִּמְהֵרָה, בְּיָמֵינוּ בְּקָרוֹב.
אֵל בְּנֵה, בְּנֵה בֵיתְךָ בְּקָרוֹב.

God is powerful, may God build a house of peace on this earth soon.

Post Game

Announcer: Now is the time for the grounds crew to come and assist with the cleaning up of the "field" (your dining room). Your seder managers will let you know if they can use some extra help to get the "field" back in shape. Maybe you will be asked to help shake out the "tarp" (tablecloth) and remove those matzah crumbs. It's time to take out the broom for a series "sweep."

Here are some questions for you, the commentator, from your co-host in the baseball seder postgame interview:

1. How do you think the Children of Israel were able to gain victory from an opponent as powerful as the Pharaoh of Egypt?
2. At the start of their journey, what went wrong for the Children of Israel?
3. What was the winning strategy of the Children of Israel?
4. What was your favorite food at the "ballpark" tonight?
5. What do you think will happen next to the Israelites when they finally enter the Land of Israel?
6. Do you think Moses, Miriam, Aaron, or Joshua was the MVP (most valuable player) in this story? Why?
7. What does baseball teach us about being on a team? How do baseball players show their individuality even when they wear the same uniform and have to work together? Are you on a team? How is being Jewish like being on a team?
8. What can you or your family do after this seder to help feed the hungry or increase freedom in the world?
9. If you could invite any baseball heroes (living or dead) to your seder, whom would you invite?
10. Why do you think so many new American immigrants in the 20th century became baseball fans?